A Note to Parents and Caregivers:

Read-it! Joke Books are for children just starting on the amazing road to reading. These fun books support the acquisition and extension of reading skills as well as a love of books.

Published by the same company that produces *Read-it!* Readers, these books introduce the question/answer and dialogue patterns that help children expand their thinking about language structure and book formats.

When sharing joke books with a child, read in short stretches. Pause often to talk about the meaning of the jokes. The question/answer and dialogue formats work well for this purpose and provide an opportunity to talk about the language and meaning of the jokes. Have the child turn the pages and point to the pictures and familiar words. When you read the jokes, have fun creating the voices of characters or emphasizing some important words. Be sure to reread favorite jokes.

There is no right or wrong way to share books with children. Find time to read with your child, and pass on the legacy of literacy.

Adria F. Klein, Ph.D.
Professor Emeritus
California State University
San Bernardino, California

Managing Editors: Bob Temple, Catherine Neitge
Creative Director: Terri Foley
Editors: Jerry Ruff, Christianne Jones
Designer: Les Tranby
Page production: Picture Window Books
The illustrations in this book were rendered digitally.

Picture Window Books
5115 Excelsior Boulevard
Suite 232
Minneapolis, MN 55416
877-845-8392
www.picturewindowbooks.com

Printed in the United States of America.

Library of Congress Cataloging-in-Publication Data
Moore, Mark, 1947-
Spooky sillies : a book of ghost jokes / by Mark Moore ;
illustrated by Anne Haberstroh.
p. cm. — (Read-it! joke books—supercharged!)
ISBN 1-4048-0630-X
1. Ghosts—Juvenile humor. 2. Wit and humor, Juvenile.
I. Title. II. Series.

PN6231.G45M66 2004
818'.602—dc22   2004007326

Spooky Sillies

A Book of Ghost Jokes

By Mark Moore • Illustrated by Anne Haberstroh

Reading Advisers:
Adria F. Klein, Ph.D.
Professor Emeritus, California State University
San Bernardino, California

Susan Kesselring, M.A., Literacy Educator
Rosemount-Apple Valley-Eagan (Minnesota) School District

PICTURE WINDOW BOOKS
Minneapolis, Minnesota

What does a father ghost say to his son when he does something good?

That's the spirit!

What do you call a staircase
in a haunted house?

A scare-case.

What do ghosts put on their
windows to keep out flies?

Screams.

How do you make a baby ghost
stop crying?

Change his sheets.

What do you call a ghost's mistake?

A boo-boo.

How do you know that a
school is haunted?

When it has school spirit.

What do ghosts like
for breakfast?

Boo-berry pancakes.

Why was the skeleton afraid
to cross the road?

*Because he didn't
have the guts.*

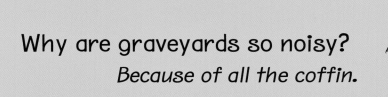

Why are graveyards so noisy?

Because of all the coffin.

Why didn't the skeleton eat
the cafeteria food?

Because he didn't have
the stomach for it.

How do ghosts keep fit?

With a scare-master.

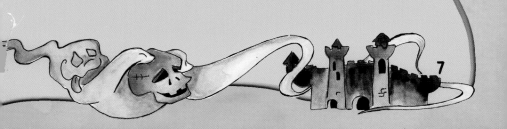

What do you call the ghost
of a turkey?

A gobble-in.

What do sad ghosts say?

Boo-hoo.

What kind of trousers do
ghosts wear?

Scaredy pants.

What do you call it when ghosts
haunt a theater?

Stage fright.

What kind of birds do
ghosts keep as pets?

Scare-crows.

What's a ghost's favorite
Chinese food?

Fright rice.

Why are ghosts such
good teachers?

*Because they go through
things again and again.*

What do you call the ghost
of a horse?

A night-mare.

Which room do ghosts
always avoid?

The living room.

What do you call a zombie and a
ghost when they are dating?

Ghoul-friend and boo-friend.

What do you get when a
ghost sits in a tree?

Petrified wood.

What do you call a ghost who works as a fashion model?

A cover ghoul.

In what position do
ghosts sleep?

>*Horror-zontal.*

Where do ghosts take their kids
when they go to work?

>*Day-scare centers.*

Nurse:

>"Doctor, there's a ghost
>waiting for an appointment."

Doctor:

>"Tell him I can't see him."

What does a skeleton order
to go?

>*Spare-ribs.*

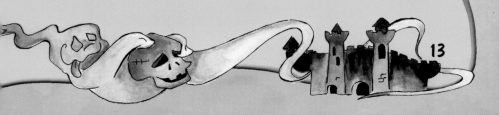

How do ghosts shave?

With shaving scream.

What is the favorite game
of baby ghosts?

Peek-a-boo.

How do ghosts like their eggs
for breakfast?

Terri-fried.

Why did the ghost love
his ghoul-friend?

*Because she was
out of sight.*

What do you do at a
ghost party?

Boo-gie.

What was the shy ghost's
biggest problem?

He didn't believe in himself.

Why was the ghost
so lonely?

Because he had no-body.

What do ghosts read
at a concert?

Sheet music.

What's a ghost's favorite
fairy tale?

Sleeping Boo-ty.

Why did the ghost stop haunting?

Because it was a dead-end job.

What do ghosts like
for breakfast?

Scream of wheat.

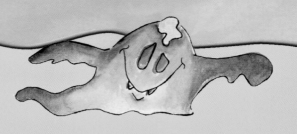

What did the cow do when she saw a ghost?

She made a milk-shake.

How do ghost parents dress their kids?

With pillowcases.

Why don't skeletons play music in church?

Because they don't have any organs.

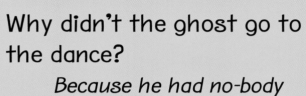

Why didn't the ghost go to the dance?

Because he had no-body to go with.

Why don't ghosts ever tell lies?

Because you can see right through them.

What do ghosts put on their bagels?

Scream cheese.

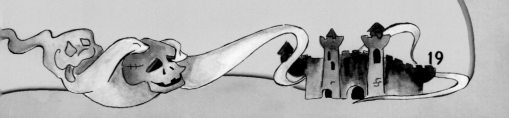

What do you call the ghost of a chicken?

A poultry-geist.

How did the skeleton know
it was going to rain?

> *He felt it in his bones.*

Where do ghosts go
for treats?

> *The I scream parlor.*

What was the baby skeleton
doing with the textbooks?

> *He was boning up for a test.*

How can you tell when
a ghost is sick?

> *He's white as a sheet.*

What ride do goblins love
at amusement parks?

The roller-ghoster.

What do they call a tired ghost
after a long night's haunting?

Dead on his feet.

What did the sheet say to
the ghost?

"I've got you covered."

What steps should you take
if a ghost is chasing you?

Big, fast ones.

Why did one skeleton chase
after the other?

*Because he had
a bone to pick.*

What kind of pets do ghosts
like best?

Scaredy cats.

Look for all of the books in this series:

Read-it! Joke Books—Supercharged!

Beastly Laughs
A Book of Monster Jokes

Roaring with Laughter
A Book of Animal Jokes

Chalkboard Chuckles
A Book of Classroom Jokes

Sit! Stay! Laugh!
A Book of Pet Jokes

Creepy Crawlers
A Book of Bug Jokes

Spooky Sillies
A Book of Ghost Jokes

Read-it! Joke Books

Alphabet Soup
A Book of Riddles About Letters

Laughs on a Leash
A Book of Pet Jokes

Animal Quack-Ups
Foolish and Funny Jokes About Animals

Monster Laughs
Frightfully Funny Jokes About Monsters

Bell Buzzers
A Book of Knock-Knock Jokes

Nutty Neighbors
A Book of Knock-Knock Jokes

Chewy Chuckles
Deliciously Funny Jokes About Food

Open Up and Laugh!
A Book of Knock-Knock Jokes

Crazy Criss-Cross
A Book of Mixed-Up Riddles

Rhyme Time
A Book of Rhyming Riddles

Ding Dong
A Book of Knock-Knock Jokes

School Buzz
Classy and Funny Jokes About School

Dino Rib Ticklers
Hugely Funny Jokes About Dinosaurs

School Daze
A Book of Riddles About School

Doctor, Doctor
A Book of Doctor Jokes

Teacher Says
A Book of Teacher Jokes

Door Knockers
A Book of Knock-Knock Jokes

Three-Alarm Jokes
A Book of Firefighter Jokes

Family Funnies
A Book of Family Jokes

Under Arrest
A Book of Police Jokes

Funny Talk
A Book of Silly Riddles

Who's There?
A Book of Knock-Knock Jokes

Galactic Giggles
Far-Out and Funny Jokes About Outer Space

Zoodles
A Book of Riddles About Animals